THE TYRANNOSAURUS DRIP SONG

Lyrics and melody by JULIA DONALDSON

Illustrations by DAVID ROBERTS

MACMILLAN CHILDREN'S BOOKS

"Drip, get a grip!" the others
keep on sneering.
"Wrong face. Out of place,"
they won't stop jeering.

"Is he a real tyrannosaurus?
Is he against us or is he for us?"

So you slip, Drip, down to the water's edge,
And you sigh as you eye the swamp of juicy veg.

You were born on the wrong side of the river,
And the other side seems so far,
And you don't know who you are.

"Eat up your meat!" the others keep on saying.
"You can't have a plant – stop disobeying.
Is he a real tyrannosaurus?
Quite frankly, Drip, you begin to bore us."

So you slip, Drip, down
to the water's edge,

And you sigh as you eye
the swamp of juicy veg.

And you stand on the
wrong side of the river,

And the other side seems so far,
And you wonder who you are.

Drip, get a grip. You know you're not a loser.
Don't stay – run away, and be a chooser.

If you're not a real tyrannosaurus,
Why should you join in the T Rex chorus?

You can slip, Drip, down to the water's edge,
But don't sigh as you eye the swamp of juicy veg.

For the time has come to swim across the river,
And the other side won't seem far,

And you'll find out who you are.

And you'll find that you're a star!

The Tyrannosaurus Drip Song

Julia Donaldson

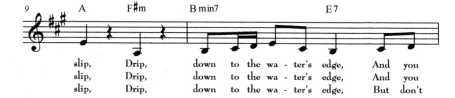

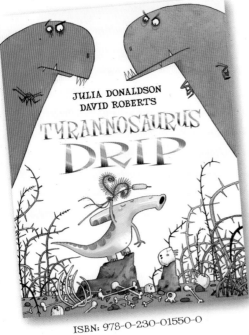